Fourth State of the Union Address

JAMES KNOX POLK

1848

TABLE OF CONTENTS

FELLOW-CITIZENS OF THE SENATE AND OF
THE HOUSE OF REPRESENTATIVES

FELLOW-CITIZENS OF THE SENATE AND OF THE HOUSE OF REPRESENTATIVES

Under the benignant providence of Almighty God the representatives of the States and of the people are again brought together to deliberate for the public good. The gratitude of the nation to the Sovereign Arbiter of All Human Events should be commensurate with the boundless blessings which we enjoy.

Peace, plenty, and contentment reign throughout our borders, and our beloved country presents a sublime moral spectacle to the world.

The troubled and unsettled condition of some of the principal European powers has had a necessary tendency to check and embarrass trade and to depress prices throughout all commercial nations, but notwithstanding these causes, the United States, with their abundant products, have felt their effects less severely than any other country, and all our great interests are still prosperous and successful.

In reviewing the great events of the past year and contrasting the agitated and disturbed state of other countries with our own tranquil and happy condition, we may congratulate ourselves that we are the most favored people on the face of the earth. While the people of other countries are struggling to establish free institutions, under which man may govern himself, we are in the actual enjoyment of them-a rich inheritance from our fathers. While enlightened nations of Europe are convulsed and distracted by civil war or intestine strife, we settle all our political controversies by the peaceful exercise of the rights of freemen at the ballot box.

The great republican maxim, so deeply engraven on the hearts of our people, that the will of the majority, constitutionally expressed, shall prevail, is our sure safeguard against force and violence. It is a subject of just pride that our fame and character as a nation continue rapidly to advance in the estimation of the civilized world.

To our wise and free institutions it is to be attributed that while other nations have achieved glory at the price of the suffering, distress, and impoverishment of their people, we have won our honorable position in the midst of an uninterrupted prosperity and of an increasing individual comfort and happiness.

I am happy to inform you that our relations with all nations are friendly and pacific. Advantageous treaties of commerce have been concluded within the last four years with New Granada, Peru, the Two Sicilies, Belgium, Hanover, Oldenburg, and Mecklenburg-Schwerin. Pursuing our example, the restrictive system of Great Britain, our principal foreign customer, has been relaxed, a more liberal commercial policy has been adopted by other enlightened nations, and our trade has been greatly enlarged and extended. Our country stands higher in the respect of the world than at any former period. To continue to occupy this proud position, it is only necessary to preserve peace and faithfully adhere to the great and fundamental principle of our foreign policy of noninterference in the domestic concerns of other nations. We recognize in all nations the right which we enjoy ourselves, to change and reform their political institutions according to their own will and pleasure. Hence we do not look behind existing governments capable of maintaining their own authority. We recognize all such actual governments, not only from the dictates of true policy, but from a sacred regard for the independence of nations. While this is our settled policy, it does not follow that we can ever be indifferent spectators of the progress of liberal principles. The Government and people of the United States hailed with enthusiasm and delight the establishment of the French Republic, as we now hail the efforts in progress to unite the States of Germany in a confederation similar in many respects to our own Federal Union. If the great and enlightened German States, occupying, as they do, a central and commanding position in Europe, shall succeed in establishing such a confederated government, securing at the same time to the citizens of each State local governments adapted to the peculiar condition of each, with unrestricted trade and intercourse with each other, it will be an important era in the history of human events. Whilst it will consolidate and strengthen the power of Germany, it must essentially promote the cause of peace, commerce, civilization, and constitutional liberty throughout the world.

With all the Governments on this continent our relations, it is believed, are now on a more friendly and satisfactory footing than they have ever been at any former period.

Since the exchange of ratifications of the treaty of peace with Mexico our intercourse with the Government of that Republic has been of the most friendly character. The envoy extraordinary and minister plenipotentiary of the United States to Mexico has been received and accredited, and a diplomatic representative from Mexico of similar rank has been received and accredited by this Government. The amicable relations between the two countries, which had been suspended, have been happily restored, and are destined, I trust, to be long preserved. The two Republics, both situated on this continent, and with coterminous territories, have every motive of sympathy and of interest to bind them together in perpetual amity.

This gratifying condition of our foreign relations renders it unnecessary for me to call your attention more specifically to them.

It has been my constant aim and desire to cultivate peace and commerce with all nations. Tranquility at home and peaceful relations abroad constitute the true permanent policy of our country. War, the scourge of nations, sometimes becomes inevitable, but is always to be avoided when it can be done consistently with the rights and honor of a nation.

One of the most important results of the war into which we were recently forced with a neighboring nation is the demonstration it has afforded of the military strength of our country. Before the late war with Mexico European and other foreign powers entertained imperfect and erroneous views of our physical strength as a nation and of our ability to prosecute war, and especially a war waged out of out own country. They saw that our standing Army on the peace establishment did not exceed 10,000 men. Accustomed themselves to maintain in peace large standing armies for the protection of thrones against their own subjects, as well as against foreign enemies, they had not conceived that it was possible for a nation without such an army, well disciplined and of long service, to wage war successfully. They held in low repute our militia, and were far from regarding them as an effective force, unless it might be for temporary defensive operations when invaded on our own soil. The events of the late war with Mexico have not only undeceived them, but have removed erroneous impressions which prevailed to some extent even among a portion of our own countrymen. That war has demonstrated that upon the breaking out of hostilities not anticipated, and for which no previous preparation had been made, a volunteer army of citizen soldiers equal to veteran troops, and in numbers equal to any emergency, can in a short period be brought into the field. Unlike what would have occurred in any other country, we were under no necessity of resorting to drafts or conscriptions. On the contrary, such was the number of volunteers who patriotically tendered their services that the chief difficulty was in making selections and determining who should be disappointed and compelled to remain at home. Our citizen soldiers are unlike those drawn from the population of any other country. They are composed indiscriminately of all professions and pursuits-of farmers, lawyers, physicians, merchants, manufacturers, mechanics, and laborers-and this not only among the officers, but the private soldiers in the ranks. Our citizen soldiers are unlike those of any other country in other respects. They are armed, and have been accustomed from their youth up to handle and use firearms, and a large proportion of them, especially in the Western and more newly settled States, are expert marksmen. They are men who have a reputation to maintain at home by their good conduct in the field. They are intelligent, and there is an individuality of character which is found in the ranks of no other army. In battle each private man, as well as every officer, rights not only for his country, but for glory and distinction among his fellow-citizens when he shall return to civil life.

The war with Mexico has demonstrated not only the ability of the Government to organize a numerous army upon a sudden call, but also to provide it with all the munitions and necessary supplies with dispatch, convenience, and ease, and to direct its operations with efficiency. The strength of our institutions has not only been displayed in the valor and skill of our troops engaged in active service in the field, but in the organization of those executive branches which were charged with the general direction and conduct of the war. While too great praise can not be bestowed upon the officers and men who fought our battles, it would be unjust to withhold from those officers necessarily stationed at home, who were charged with the duty of furnishing the Army in proper time and at proper places with all the munitions of war and other supplies so necessary to make it efficient, the commendation to which they are entitled. The credit due to this class of our officers is the greater when it is considered that no army in ancient or modern times was even better appointed or provided than our Army in Mexico. Operating in an enemy's country, removed 2,000 miles from the seat of the Federal Government, its different corps spread over a vast extent of territory, hundreds and even thousands of miles apart from each other, nothing short of the untiring vigilance and extraordinary energy of these officers could have enabled them to provide the Army at all points and in proper season with all that was required for the most efficient service.

It is but an act of justice to declare that the officers in charge of the several executive bureaus, all under the immediate eye and supervision of the Secretary of War, performed their respective duties with ability, energy, and efficiency. They have reaped less of the glory of the war, not having been personally exposed to its perils in battle, than their companions in arms; but without their forecast, efficient aid, and cooperation those in the field would not have been provided with the ample means they possessed of achieving for themselves and their country the unfading honors which they have won for both.

When all these facts are considered, it may cease to be a matter of so much amazement abroad how it happened that our noble Army in Mexico, regulars and volunteers, were victorious upon every battlefield, however fearful the odds against them.

The war with Mexico has thus fully developed the capacity of republican governments to prosecute successfully a just and necessary foreign war with all the vigor usually attributed to more arbitrary forms of government. It has been usual for writers on public law to impute to republics a want of that unity, concentration of purpose, and vigor of execution which are generally admitted to belong to the monarchical and aristocratic forms; and this feature of popular government has been supposed to display itself more particularly in the conduct of a war carried on in an enemy's territory. The war with Great Britain in 1812 was to a great extent confined within our own limits, and shed but little light on this subject; but the war which we have just closed by an honorable peace evinces beyond all doubt that a popular representative government is equal to any emergency which is likely to arise in the affairs of a nation.

The war with Mexico has developed most strikingly and conspicuously another feature in our institutions. It is that without cost to the Government or danger to our liberties we have in the bosom of our society of freemen, available in a just and necessary war, virtually a standing army of 2,000,000 armed citizen soldiers, such as fought the battles of Mexico. But our military strength does not consist alone in our capacity for extended and successful operations on land. The Navy is an important arm of the national defense. If the services of the Navy were not so brilliant as those of the Army in the late war with Mexico, it was because they had no enemy to meet on their own element. While the Army had opportunity of performing more conspicuous service, the Navy largely participated in the conduct of the war. Both branches of the service performed their whole duty to the country. For the able and gallant services of the officers and men of the Navy, acting independently as well as in cooperation with our troops, in the conquest of the Californias, the capture of Vera Cruz, and the seizure and occupation of other important positions on the Gulf and Pacific coasts, the highest praise is due. Their vigilance, energy, and skill rendered the most effective service in excluding munitions of war and other supplies from the enemy, while they secured a safe entrance for abundant supplies for our own Army. Our extended commerce was nowhere interrupted, and for this immunity from the evils of war the country is indebted to the Navy.

High praise is due to the officers of the several executive bureaus, navy-yards, and stations connected with the service, all under the immediate direction of the Secretary of the Navy, for the industry, foresight, and energy with which everything was directed and furnished to give efficiency to that branch of the service. The same vigilance existed in directing the operations of the Navy as of the Army. There was concert of action and of purpose between the heads of the two arms of the service. By the orders which were from time to time issued, our vessels of war on the Pacific and the Gulf of Mexico were stationed in proper time and in proper positions to cooperate efficiently with the Army. By this means their combined power was brought to bear successfully on the enemy.

The great results which have been developed and brought to light by this war will be of immeasurable importance in the future progress of our country. They will tend powerfully to preserve us from foreign collisions, and to enable us to pursue uninterruptedly our cherished policy of "peace with all nations, entangling alliances with none."

Occupying, as we do, a more commanding position among nations than at any former period, our duties and our responsibilities to ourselves and to posterity are correspondingly increased. This will be the more obvious when we consider the vast additions which have been recently made to our territorial possessions and their great importance and value.

Within less than four years the annexation of Texas to the Union has been consummated; all conflicting title to the Oregon Territory south of the forty-ninth degree of north latitude, being all that was insisted on by any of my predecessors, has been adjusted, and New Mexico and Upper California have been acquired by treaty. The area of these several Territories, according to a report carefully prepared by the Commissioner of the General Land Office from the most authentic information in his possession, and which is herewith transmitted, contains 1,193,061 square miles, or 763,559,040 acres; while the area of the remaining twenty-nine

States and the territory not yet organized into States east of the Rocky Mountains contains 2,059,513 square miles, or 1,318,126,058 acres. These estimates show that the territories recently acquired, and over which our exclusive jurisdiction and dominion have been extended, constitute a country more than half as large as all that which was held by the United States before their acquisition. If Oregon be excluded from the estimate, there will still remain within the limits of Texas, New Mexico, and California 851,598 square miles, or 545,012,720 acres, being an addition equal to more than one-third of all the territory owned by the United States before their acquisition, and, including Oregon, nearly as great an extent of territory as the whole of Europe, Russia only excepted. The Mississippi, so lately the frontier of our country, is now only its center. With the addition of the late acquisitions, the United States are now estimated to be nearly as large as the whole of Europe. It is estimated by the Superintendent of the Coast Survey in the accompanying report that the extent of the seacoast of Texas on the Gulf of Mexico is upward of 400 miles; of the coast of Upper California on the Pacific, of 970 miles, and of Oregon, including the Straits of Fuca, of 650 miles, making the whole extent of seacoast on the Pacific 1,620 miles and the whole extent on both the Pacific and the Gulf of Mexico 2,020 miles. The length of the coast on the Atlantic from the northern limits of the United States around the capes of Florida to the Sabine, on the eastern boundary of Texas, is estimated to be 3,100 miles; so that the addition of seacoast, including Oregon, is very nearly two-thirds as great as all we possessed before, and, excluding Oregon, is an addition of 1,370 miles, being nearly equal to one-half of the extent of coast which we possessed before these acquisitions. We have now three great maritime fronts-on the Atlantic, the Gulf of Mexico, and the Pacific-making in the whole an extent of seacoast exceeding 5,000 miles. This is the extent of the seacoast of the United States, not including bays, sounds, and small irregularities of the main shore and of the sea islands. If these be included, the length of the shore line of coast, as estimated by the Superintendent of the Coast Survey in his report, would be 33,063 miles.

It would be difficult to calculate the value of these immense additions to our territorial possessions. Texas, lying contiguous to the western boundary of Louisiana, embracing within its limits a part of the navigable tributary waters of the Mississippi and an extensive seacoast, could not long have remained in the hands of a foreign power without endangering the peace of our southwestern frontier. Her products in the vicinity of the tributaries of the Mississippi must have sought a market through these streams, running into and through our territory, and the danger of irritation and collision of interests between Texas as a foreign state and ourselves would have been imminent, while the embarrassments in the commercial intercourse between them must have been constant and unavoidable. Had Texas fallen into the hands or under the influence and control of a strong maritime or military foreign power, as she might have done, these dangers would have been still greater. They have been avoided by her voluntary and peaceful annexation to the United States. Texas, from her position, was a natural and almost indispensable part of our territories. Fortunately, she has been restored to our country, and now constitutes one of the States of our Confederacy, "upon an equal footing with the original States." The salubrity of climate, the fertility of soil, peculiarly adapted to the production of some of our most valuable staple commodities, and her commercial advantages must soon make her one of our most populous States.

New Mexico, though situated in the interior and without a seacoast, is known to contain much fertile land, to abound in rich mines of the precious metals, and to be capable of sustaining a large population. From its position it is the intermediate and connecting territory between our settlements and our possessions in Texas and those on the Pacific Coast.

Upper California, irrespective of the vast mineral wealth recently developed there, holds at this day, in point of value and importance, to the rest of the Union the same relation that Louisiana did when that fine territory was acquired from France forty-five years ago. Extending nearly ten degrees of latitude along the Pacific, and embracing the only safe and commodious harbors on that coast for many hundred miles, with a temperate climate and an extensive interior of fertile lands, it is scarcely possible to estimate its wealth until it shall be brought under the government of our laws and its resources fully developed. From its position it must command the rich commerce of China, of Asia, of the islands of the Pacific, of western Mexico, of Central America, the South American States, and of the Russian possessions bordering on that ocean. A great emporium will doubtless speedily arise on the Californian coast which may be destined to rival in importance New Orleans itself. The depot of the vast commerce which must exist on the Pacific will probably be at some point on the Bay of San Francisco, and will occupy the same relation to the whole western coast of that ocean as New Orleans does to the valley of the Mississippi and the Gulf of Mexico. To this depot our numerous whale ships will resort with their cargoes to trade, refit, and obtain supplies. This of itself will largely contribute to build up a city, which would soon become the center of a great and rapidly increasing commerce. Situated on a safe harbor, sufficiently capacious for all the navies as well as the marine of the world, and convenient to excellent timber for shipbuilding, owned by the United States, it must become our great Western naval depot.

It was known that mines of the precious metals existed to a considerable extent in California at the time of its acquisition. Recent discoveries render it probable that these mines are more extensive and valuable than was anticipated. The accounts of the abundance of gold in that territory are of such an extraordinary character as would scarcely command belief were they not corroborated by the authentic reports of officers in the public service who have visited the mineral district and derived the facts which they detail from personal observation. Reluctant to credit the reports in general circulation as to the quantity of gold, the officer commanding our forces in California visited the mineral district in July last for the purpose of obtaining accurate information on the subject. His report to the War Department of the result of his examination and the facts obtained on the spot is herewith laid before Congress. When he visited the country there were about 4,000 persons engaged in collecting gold. There is every reason to believe that the number of persons so employed has since been augmented. The explorations already made warrant the belief that the supply is very large and that gold is found at various places in an extensive district of country.

Information received from officers of the Navy and other sources, though not so full and minute, confirms the accounts of the commander of our military force in California. It appears also from these reports that mines of quicksilver are found in the vicinity of the gold region. One of them is now being worked, and is believed to be among the most productive in the world.

The effects produced by the discovery of these rich mineral deposits and the success which has attended the labors of those who have resorted to them have produced a surprising change in the state of affairs in California. Labor commands a most exorbitant price, and all other pursuits but that of searching for the precious metals are abandoned. Nearly the whole of the male population of the country have gone to the gold districts. Ships arriving on the coast are deserted by their crews and their voyages suspended for want of sailors. Our commanding officer there entertains apprehensions that soldiers can not be kept in the public service without a large increase of pay. Desertions in his command have become frequent, and he recommends that those who shall withstand the strong temptation and remain faithful should be rewarded.

This abundance of gold and the all-engrossing pursuit of it have already caused in California an unprecedented rise in the price of all the necessaries of life.

That we may the more speedily and fully avail ourselves of the undeveloped wealth of these mines, it is deemed of vast importance that a branch of the Mint of the United States be authorized to be established at your present session in California. Among other signal advantages which would result from such an establishment would be that of raising the gold to its par value in that territory. A branch mint of the United States at the great commercial depot on the west coast would convert into our own coin not only the gold derived from our own rich mines, but also the bullion and specie which our commerce may bring from the whole west coast of Central and South America. The west coast of America and the adjacent interior embrace the richest and best mines of Mexico, New Granada, Central America, Chili, and Peru. The bullion and specie drawn from these countries, and especially from those of western Mexico and Peru, to an amount in value of many millions of dollars, are now annually diverted and carried by the ships of Great Britain to her own ports, to be recoined or used to sustain her national bank, and thus contribute to increase her ability to command so much of the commerce of the world. If a branch mint be established at the great commercial point upon that coast, a vast amount of bullion and specie would flow thither to be recoined, and pass thence to New Orleans, New York, and other Atlantic cities. The amount of our constitutional currency at home would be greatly increased, while its circulation abroad would be promoted. It is well known to our merchants trading to China and the west coast of America that great inconvenience and loss are experienced from the fact that our coins are not current at their par value in those countries.

The powers of Europe, far removed from the west coast of America by the Atlantic Ocean, which intervenes, and by a tedious and dangerous navigation around the southern cape of the continent of America, can never successfully compete with the United States in the rich and extensive commerce which is opened to us at so much less cost by the acquisition of California.

The vast importance and commercial advantages of California have heretofore remained undeveloped by the Government of the country of which it constituted a part. Now that this fine province is a part of our country, all the States of the Union, some more immediately and directly than others, are deeply interested in the speedy development of its wealth and resources. No section of our country is more interested or will be more benefited than the commercial, navigating, and manufacturing interests of the Eastern States. Our planting and farming interests in every part of the Union will Be greatly benefited by it. As our commerce and navigation are enlarged and extended, our exports of agricultural products and of manufactures will be increased, and in the new markets thus opened they can not fail to command remunerating and profitable prices.

The acquisition of California and New Mexico, the settlement of the Oregon boundary, and the annexation of Texas, extending to the Rio Grande, are results which, combined, are of greater consequence and will add more to the strength and wealth of the nation than any which have preceded them since the adoption of the Constitution.

But to effect these great results not only California, but New Mexico, must be brought under the control of regularly organized governments. The existing condition of California and of that part of New Mexico lying west of the Rio Grande and without the limits of Texas imperiously demands that Congress should at its present session organize Territorial governments over them.

Upon the exchange of ratifications of the treaty of peace with Mexico, on the 30th of May last, the temporary governments which had been established over New Mexico and California by our military and naval commanders by virtue of the rights of war ceased to derive any obligatory force from that source of authority, and having been ceded to the United States, all government and control over them under the authority of Mexico had ceased to exist. Impressed with the necessity of establishing Territorial governments over them, I recommended the subject to the favorable consideration of Congress in my message communicating the ratified treaty of peace, on the 6th of July last, and invoked their action at that session. Congress adjourned without making any provision for their government. The inhabitants by the transfer of their country had become entitled to the benefit of our laws and Constitution, and yet were left without any regularly organized government. Since that time the very limited power possessed by the Executive has been exercised to preserve and protect them from the inevitable consequences of a state of anarchy. The only government which remained was that established by the military authority during the war. Regarding this to be a de facto government, and that by the presumed consent of the inhabitants it might be continued temporarily, they were advised to conform and submit to it for the short intervening period before Congress would again assemble and could legislate on the subject. The views entertained by the Executive on this point are contained in a communication of the Secretary of State dated the 7th of October last, which was forwarded for publication to California and New Mexico, a copy of which is herewith transmitted. The small military force of the Regular Army which was serving within the limits of the acquired territories at the close of the war was retained in them, and additional forces have been ordered there for the protection of the inhabitants and to preserve and secure the rights and interests of the United States.

No revenue has been or could be collected at the ports in California, because Congress failed to authorize the establishment of custom-houses or the appointment of officers for that purpose.

The Secretary of the Treasury, by a circular letter addressed to collectors of the customs on the 7th day of October last, a copy of which is herewith transmitted, exercised all the power with which he was invested by law.

In pursuance of the act of the 14th of August last, extending the benefit of our post-office laws to the people of California, the Postmaster-General has appointed two agents, who have proceeded, the one to California and the other to Oregon, with authority to make the necessary arrangements for carrying its provisions into effect.

The monthly line of mail steamers from Panama to Astoria has been required to "stop and deliver and take mails at San Diego, Monterey, and San Francisco." These mail steamers, connected by the Isthmus of Panama with the line of mail steamers on the Atlantic between New York and Chagres, will establish a regular mail communication with California.

It is our solemn duty to provide with the least practicable delay for New Mexico and California regularly organized Territorial governments. The causes of the failure to do this at the last session of Congress are well known and deeply to be regretted. With the opening prospects of increased prosperity and national greatness which the acquisition of these rich and extensive territorial possessions affords, how irrational it would be to forego or to reject these advantages by the agitation of a domestic question which is coeval with the existence of our Government itself, and to endanger by internal strifes, geographical divisions, and heated contests for political power, or for any other cause, the harmony of the glorious Union of our confederated States-that Union which binds us together as one people, and which for sixty years has been our shield and protection against every danger. In the eyes of the world and of posterity how trivial and insignificant will be all our internal divisions and struggles compared with the preservation of this Union of the States in all its vigor and with all its countless blessings! No patriot would foment and excite geographical and sectional divisions. No lover of his country would deliberately calculate the value of the Union. Future generations would look in amazement upon the folly of such a course. Other nations at the present day would look upon it with astonishment, and such of them as desire to maintain and perpetuate thrones and monarchical or aristocratical principles will view it with exultation and delight, because in it they will see the elements of faction, which they hope must ultimately overturn our system. Ours is the great example of a prosperous and free self-governed republic, commanding the admiration and the imitation of all the lovers of freedom throughout the world. How solemn, therefore, is the duty, how impressive the call upon us and upon all parts of our country, to cultivate a patriotic spirit of harmony, of good-fellowship, of compromise and mutual concession, in the administration of the incomparable system of government formed by our fathers in the midst of almost insuperable difficulties, and transmitted to us with the injunction that we should enjoy its blessings and hand it down unimpaired to those who may come after us.

In view of the high and responsible duties which we owe to ourselves and to mankind, I trust you may be able at your present session to approach the adjustment of the only domestic question which seriously threatens, or probably ever can threaten, to disturb the harmony and successful operations of our system.

The immensely valuable possessions of New Mexico and California are already inhabited by a considerable population. Attracted by their great fertility, their mineral wealth, their commercial advantages, and the salubrity of the climate, emigrants from the older States in great numbers are already preparing to seek new homes in these inviting regions. Shall the dissimilarity of the domestic institutions in the different States prevent us from providing for them suitable governments? These institutions existed at the adoption of the Constitution, but the obstacles which they interposed were overcome by that spirit of compromise which is now invoked. In a conflict of opinions or of interests, real or imaginary, between different sections of our country, neither can justly demand all which it might desire to obtain. Each, in the true spirit of our institutions, should concede something to the other.

Our gallant forces in the Mexican war, by whose patriotism and unparalleled deeds of arms we obtained these possessions as an indemnity for our just demands against Mexico, were composed of citizens who belonged to no one State or section of our Union. They were men from slaveholding and nonslaveholding States, from the North and the South, from the East and the West. They were all companions in arms and fellow-citizens of the same common country, engaged in the same common cause. When prosecuting that war they were brethren and friends, and shared alike with each other common toils, dangers, and sufferings. Now, when their work is ended, when peace is restored, and they return again to their homes,

17

put off the habiliments of war, take their places in society, and resume their pursuits in civil life, surely a spirit of harmony and concession and of equal regard for the rights of all and of all sections of the Union ought to prevail in providing governments for the acquired territories-the fruits of their common service. The whole people of the United States, and of every State, contributed to defray the expenses of that war, and it would not be just for any one section to exclude another from all participation in the acquired territory. This would not be in consonance with the just system of government which the framers of the Constitution adopted.

The question is believed to be rather abstract than practical whether slavery ever can or would exist in any portion of the acquired territory even if it were left to the option of the slaveholding States themselves. From the nature of the climate and productions in much the larger portion of it it is certain it could never exist, and in the remainder the probabilities are it would not. But however this may be, the question, involving, as it does, a principle of equality of rights of the separate and several States as equal copartners in the Confederacy, should not be disregarded.

In organizing governments over these territories no duty imposed on Congress by the Constitution requires that they should legislate on the subject of slavery, while their power to do so is not only seriously questioned, but denied by many of the soundest expounders of that instrument. Whether Congress shall legislate or not, the people of the acquired territories, when assembled in convention to form State constitutions, will possess the sole and exclusive power to determine for themselves whether slavery shall or shall not exist within their limits. If Congress shall abstain from interfering with the question, the people of these territories will be left free to adjust it as they may think proper when they apply for admission as States into the Union. No enactment of Congress could restrain the people of any of the sovereign States of the Union, old or new, North or South, slaveholding or nonslaveholding, from determining the character of their own domestic institutions as they may deem wise and proper. Any and all the States possess this right, and Congress can not deprive them of it. The people of Georgia might if they chose so alter their constitution as to abolish slavery within its limits, and the people of Vermont might so alter their constitution as to admit slavery within its limits. Both States would possess the right, though, as all know, it is not probable that either would exert it.

It is fortunate for the peace and harmony of the Union that this question is in its nature temporary and can only continue for the brief period which will intervene before California and New Mexico may be admitted as States into the Union. From the tide of population now flowing into them it is highly probable that this will soon occur.

Considering the several States and the citizens of the several States as equals and entitled to equal rights under the Constitution, if this were an original question it might well be insisted on that the principle of noninterference is the true doctrine and that Congress could not, in the absence of any express grant of power, interfere with their relative rights. Upon a great emergency, however, and under menacing dangers to the Union, the Missouri compromise line in respect to slavery was adopted. The same line was extended farther west in the acquisition of Texas. After an acquiescence of nearly thirty years in the principle of compromise recognized and established by these acts, and to avoid the danger to the Union which might follow if it were now disregarded, I have heretofore expressed the opinion that that line of compromise should be extended on the parallel of 36° 30' from the western boundary of Texas, where it now terminates, to the Pacific Ocean. This is the middle ground of compromise, upon which the different sections of the Union may meet, as they have heretofore met. If this be done, it is confidently believed a large majority of the people of every section of the country, however widely their abstract opinions on the subject of slavery may differ, would cheerfully and patriotically acquiesce in it, and peace and harmony would again fill our borders.

The restriction north of the line was only yielded to in the case of Missouri and Texas upon a principle of compromise, made necessary for the sake of preserving the harmony and possibly the existence of the Union.

It was upon these considerations that at the close of your last session I gave my sanction to the principle of the Missouri compromise line by approving and signing the bill to establish "the Territorial government of Oregon." From a sincere desire to preserve the harmony of the Union, and in deference for the acts of my predecessors, I felt constrained to yield my acquiescence to the extent to which they had gone in compromising this delicate and dangerous question. But if Congress shall now reverse the decision by which the Missouri compromise was effected, and shall propose to extend the restriction over the whole territory, south as well as north of the parallel of 36° 30', it will cease to be a compromise, and must be regarded as an original question.

If Congress, instead of observing the course of noninterference, leaving the adoption of their own domestic institutions to the people who may inhabit these territories, or if, instead of extending the Missouri compromise line to the Pacific, shall prefer to submit the legal and constitutional questions which may arise to the decision of the judicial tribunals, as was proposed in a bill which passed the Senate at your last session, an adjustment may be effected in this mode. If the whole subject be referred to the judiciary, all parts of the Union should cheerfully acquiesce in the final decision of the tribunal created by the Constitution for the settlement of all questions which may arise under the Constitution, treaties, and laws of the United States.

Congress is earnestly invoked, for the sake of the Union, its harmony, and our continued prosperity as a nation, to adjust at its present session this, the only dangerous question which lies in our path, if not in some one of the modes suggested, in some other which may be satisfactory.

In anticipation of the establishment of regular governments over the acquired territories, a joint commission of officers of the Army and Navy has been ordered to proceed to the coast of California and Oregon for the purpose of making reconnoissances and a report as to the proper sites for the erection of fortifications or other defensive works on land and of suitable situations for naval stations. The information which may be expected from a scientific and skillful examination of the whole face of the coast will be eminently useful to Congress when they come to consider the propriety of making appropriations for these great national objects. Proper defenses on land will be necessary for the security and protection of our possessions, and the establishment of navy-yards and a dock for the repair and construction of vessels will be important alike to our Navy and commercial marine. Without such establishments every vessel, whether of the Navy or of the merchant service, requiring repair must at great expense come round Cape Horn to one of our Atlantic yards for that purpose. With such establishments vessels, it is believed may be built or repaired as cheaply in California as upon the Atlantic coast. They would give employment to many of our enterprising shipbuilders and mechanics and greatly facilitate and enlarge our commerce in the Pacific.

As it is ascertained that mines of gold, silver, copper, and quicksilver exist in New Mexico and California, and that nearly all the lands where they are found belong to the United States, it is deemed important to the public interest that provision be made for a geological and mineralogical examination of these regions. Measures should be adopted to preserve the mineral lands, especially such as contain the precious metals, for the use of the United States, or, if brought into market, to separate them from the farming lands and dispose of them in such manner as to secure a large return of money to the Treasury and at the same time to lead to the development of their wealth by individual proprietors and purchasers. To do this it will be necessary to provide for an immediate survey and location of the lots. If Congress should deem it proper to dispose of the mineral lands, they should be sold in small quantities and at a fixed minimum price.

I recommend that surveyors-general's offices be authorized to be established in New Mexico and California and provision made for surveying and bringing the public lands into market at the earliest practicable period. In disposing of these lands, I recommend that the right of preemption be secured and liberal grants made to the early emigrants who have settled or may settle upon them.

It will be important to extend our revenue laws over these territories, and especially over California, at an early period. There is already a considerable commerce with California, and until ports of entry shall be established and collectors appointed no revenue can be received.

If these and other necessary and proper measures be adopted for the development of the wealth and resources of New Mexico and California and regular Territorial governments be established over them, such will probably be the rapid enlargement of our commerce and navigation and such the addition to the national wealth that the present generation may live to witness the controlling commercial and monetary power of the world transferred from London and other European emporiums to the city of New York.

The apprehensions which were entertained by some of our statesmen in the earlier periods of the Government that our system was incapable of operating with sufficient energy and success over largely extended territorial limits, and that if this were attempted it would fall to pieces by its own weakness, have been dissipated by our experience. By the division of power between the States and Federal Government the latter is found to operate with as much energy in the extremes as in the center. It is as efficient in the remotest of the thirty States which now compose the Union as it was in the thirteen States which formed our Constitution. Indeed, it may well be doubted whether if our present population had been confined within the limits of the original thirteen States the tendencies to centralization and consolidation would not have been such as to have encroached upon the essential reserved rights of the States, and thus to have made the Federal Government a widely different one, practically, from what it is in theory and was intended to be by its framers. So far from entertaining apprehensions of the safety of our system by the extension of our territory, the belief is confidently entertained that each new State gives strength and an additional guaranty for the preservation of the Union itself.

In pursuance of the provisions of the thirteenth article of the treaty of peace, friendship, limits, and settlement with the Republic of Mexico, and of the act of July 29, 1848, claims of our citizens, which had been "already liquidated and decided, against the Mexican Republic" amounting, with the interest thereon, to $2,023,832.51 have been liquidated and paid. There remain to be paid of these claims $74,192.26.

Congress at its last session having made no provision for executing the fifteenth article of the treaty, by which the United States assume to make satisfaction for the "unliquidated claims" of our citizens against Mexico to "an amount not exceeding three and a quarter millions of dollars," the subject is again recommended to your favorable consideration.

The exchange of ratifications of the treaty with Mexico took place on the 30th of May, 1848. Within one year after that time the commissioner and surveyor which each Government stipulates to appoint are required to meet "at the port of San Diego and proceed to run and mark the said boundary in its whole course to the mouth of the Rio Bravo del Norte." It will be seen from this provision that the period within which a commissioner and surveyor of the respective Governments are to meet at San Diego will expire on the 30th of May, 1849. Congress at the close of its last session made an appropriation for "the expenses of running and marking the boundary line" between the two countries, but did not fix the amount of salary which should be paid to the commissioner and surveyor to be appointed on the part of the United States. It is desirable that the amount of compensation which they shall receive should be prescribed by law, and not left, as at present, to Executive discretion.

Measures were adopted at the earliest practicable period to organize the "Territorial government of Oregon," as authorized by the act of the 14th of August last. The governor and marshal of the Territory, accompanied by a small military escort, left the frontier of Missouri in September last, and took the southern route, by the way of Santa Fe and the river Gila, to California, with the intention of proceeding thence in one of our vessels of war to their destination. The governor was fully advised of the great importance of his early arrival in the country, and it is confidently believed he may reach Oregon in the latter part of the present month or early in the next. The other officers for the Territory have proceeded by sea.

In the month of May last I communicated information to Congress that an Indian war had broken out in Oregon, and recommended that authority be given to raise an adequate number of volunteers to proceed without delay to the assistance of our fellow-citizens in that Territory. The authority to raise such a force not having been granted by Congress, as soon as their services could be dispensed with in Mexico orders were issued to the regiment of mounted riflemen to proceed to Jefferson Barracks, in Missouri, and to prepare to march to Oregon as soon as the necessary provision could be made. Shortly before it was ready to march it was arrested by the provision of the act passed by Congress on the last day of the last session, which directed that all the noncommissioned officers, musicians, and privates of that regiment who had been in service in Mexico should, upon their application, be entitled to be discharged. The effect of this provision was to disband the rank and file of the regiment, and before their places could be filled by recruits the season had so far advanced that it was impracticable for it to proceed until the opening of the next spring.

In the month of October last the accompanying communication was received from the governor of the temporary government of Oregon, giving information of the continuance of the Indian disturbances and of the destitution and defenseless condition of the inhabitants. Orders were immediately transmitted to the commander of our squadron in the Pacific to dispatch to their assistance a part of the naval forces on that station, to furnish them with arms and ammunition, and to continue to give them such aid and protection as the Navy could afford until the Army could reach the country.

It is the policy of humanity, and one which has always been pursued by the United States, to cultivate the good will of the aboriginal tribes of this continent and to restrain them from making war and indulging in excesses by mild means rather than by force. That this could have been done with the tribes in Oregon had that Territory been brought under the government of our laws at an earlier period, and had other suitable measures been adopted by Congress, such as now exist in our intercourse with the other Indian tribes within our limits, can not be doubted. Indeed, the immediate and only cause of the existing hostility of the Indians of Oregon is represented to have been the long delay of the United States in making to them some trifling compensation, in such articles as they wanted, for the country now occupied by our emigrants, which the Indians claimed and over which they formerly roamed. This compensation had been promised to them by the temporary government established in Oregon, but its fulfillment had been postponed from time to time for nearly two years, whilst those who made it had been anxiously waiting for Congress to establish a Territorial government over the country. The Indians became at length distrustful of their good faith and sought redress by plunder and massacre, which finally led to the present difficulties. A few thousand dollars in suitable presents, as a compensation for the country which had been taken possession of by our citizens, would have satisfied the Indians and have prevented the war. A small amount properly distributed, it is confidently believed, would soon restore quiet. In this Indian war our fellow-citizens of Oregon have been compelled to take the field in their own defense, have performed valuable military services, and been subjected to expenses which have fallen heavily upon them. Justice demands that provision should be made by Congress to compensate them for their services and to refund to them the necessary expenses which they have incurred.

I repeat the recommendation heretofore made to Congress, that provision be made for the appointment of a suitable number of Indian agents to reside among the tribes of Oregon, and that a small sum be appropriated to enable these agents to cultivate friendly relations with them. If this be done, the presence of a small military force will be all that is necessary to keep them in check and preserve peace. I recommend that similar provisions be made as regards the tribes inhabiting northern Texas, New Mexico, California, and the extensive region lying between our settlements in Missouri and these possessions, as the most effective means of preserving peace upon our borders and within the recently acquired territories.

The Secretary of the Treasury will present in his annual report a highly satisfactory statement of the condition of the finances.

The imports for the fiscal year ending on the 30th of June last were of the value of $154,977,876, of which the amount exported was $21,128,010, leaving $133,849,866 in the country for domestic use. The value of the exports for the same period was $154,032,131, consisting of domestic productions amounting to $132,904,121 and $21,128,010 of foreign articles. The receipts into the Treasury for the same period, exclusive of loans, amounted to $35,436,750.59, of which there was derived from customs $31,757,070.96, from sales of public lands $3,328,642.56, and from miscellaneous and incidental sources $351,037.07.

It will be perceived that the revenue from customs for the last fiscal year exceeded by $757,070.96 the estimate of the Secretary of the Treasury in his last annual report, and that the aggregate receipts during the same period from customs, lands, and miscellaneous sources also exceeded the estimate by the sum of $536,750.59, indicating, however, a very near approach in the estimate to the actual result.

The expenditures during the fiscal year ending on the 30th of June last, including those for the war and exclusive of payments of principal and interest for the public debt, were $42,811,970.03.

It is estimated that the receipts into the Treasury for the fiscal year ending on the 30th of June, 1849, including the balance in the Treasury on the 1st of July last, will amount to the sum of $57,048,969.90, of which $32,000,000, it is estimated, will be derived from customs, $3,000,000 from the sales of the public lands, and $1,200,000 from miscellaneous and incidental sources, including the premium upon the loan, and the amount paid and to be paid into the Treasury on account of military contributions in Mexico, and the sales of arms and vessels and other public property rendered unnecessary for the use of the Government by the termination of the war, and $20,695,435.30 from loans already negotiated, including Treasury notes funded, which, together with the balance in the Treasury on the 1st of July last, make the sum estimated.

The expenditures for the same period, including the necessary payment on account of the principal and interest of the public debt, and the principal and interest of the first installment due to Mexico on the 30th of May next, and other expenditures growing out of the war to be paid during the present year, will amount, including the reimbursement of Treasury notes, to the sum of $54,195,275.06, leaving an estimated balance in the Treasury on the 1st of July, 1849, of $2,853,694.84.

The Secretary of the Treasury will present, as required by law, the estimate of the receipts and expenditures for the next fiscal year. The expenditures as estimated for that year are $33,213,152.73, including $3,799,102.18 for the interest on the public debt and $3,540,000 for the principal and interest due to Mexico on the 30th of May, 1850, leaving the sum of $25,874,050.35, which, it is believed, will be ample for the ordinary peace expenditures.

The operations of the tariff act of 1846 have been such during the past year as fully to meet the public expectation and to confirm the opinion heretofore expressed of the wisdom of the change in our revenue system which was effected by it. The receipts under it into the Treasury for the first fiscal year after its enactment exceeded by the sum of $5,044,403.09 the amount collected during the last fiscal year under the tariff act of 1842, ending the 30th of June, 1846. The total revenue realized from the commencement of its operation, on the 1st of December, 1846, until the close of the last quarter, on the 30th of September last, being twenty-two months, was $56,654,563.79, being a much larger sum than was ever before received from duties during any equal period under the tariff acts of 1824, 1828, 1832, and 1842. Whilst by the repeal of highly protective and prohibitory duties the revenue has been increased, the taxes on the people have been diminished. They have been relieved from the heavy amounts with which they were burthened under former laws in the form of increased prices or bounties paid to favored classes and pursuits.

The predictions which were made that the tariff act of 1846 would reduce the amount of revenue below that collected under the act of 1842, and would prostrate the business and destroy the prosperity of the country, have not been verified. With an increased and increasing revenue, the finances are in a highly flourishing condition. Agriculture, commerce, and navigation are prosperous; the prices of manufactured fabrics and of other products are much less injuriously affected than was to have been anticipated from the unprecedented revulsions which during the last and the present year have overwhelmed the industry and paralyzed the credit and commerce of so many great and enlightened nations of Europe.

Severe commercial revulsions abroad have always heretofore operated to depress and often to affect disastrously almost every branch of American industry. The temporary depression of a portion of our manufacturing interests is the effect of foreign causes, and is far less severe than has prevailed on all former similar occasions.

It is believed that, looking to the great aggregate of all our interests, the whole country was never more prosperous than at the present period, and never more rapidly advancing in wealth and population. Neither the foreign war in which we have been involved, nor the loans which have absorbed so large a portion of our capital, nor the commercial revulsion in Great Britain in 1847, nor the paralysis of credit and commerce throughout Europe in 1848, have affected injuriously to any considerable extent any of the great interests of the country or arrested our onward march to greatness, wealth, and power.

Had the disturbances in Europe not occurred, our commerce would undoubtedly have been still more extended, and would have added still more to the national wealth and public prosperity. But notwithstanding these disturbances, the operations of the revenue system established by the tariff act of 1846 have been so generally beneficial to the Government and the business of the country that no change in its provisions is demanded by a wise public policy, and none is recommended.

The operations of the constitutional treasury established by the act of the 6th of August, 1846, in the receipt, custody, and disbursement of the public money have continued to be successful. Under this system the public finances have been carried through a foreign war, involving the necessity of loans and extraordinary expenditures and requiring distant transfers and disbursements, without embarrassment, and no loss has occurred of any of the public money deposited under its provisions. Whilst it has proved to be safe and useful to the Government, its effects have been most beneficial upon the business of the country. It has tended powerfully to secure an exemption from that inflation and fluctuation of the paper currency so injurious to domestic industry and rendering so uncertain the rewards of labor, and, it is believed, has largely contributed to preserve the whole country from a serious commercial revulsion, such as often occurred under the bank deposit system. In the year 1847 there was a revulsion in the business of Great Britain of great extent and intensity, which was followed by failures in that Kingdom unprecedented in number and amount of losses. This is believed to be the first instance when such disastrous bankruptcies, occurring in a country with which we have such extensive commerce, produced little or no injurious effect upon our trade or currency. We remained but little affected in our money market, and our business and industry were still prosperous and progressive.

During the present year nearly the whole continent of Europe has been convulsed by civil war and revolutions, attended by numerous bankruptcies, by an unprecedented fall in their public securities, and an almost universal paralysis of commerce and industry; and yet, although our trade and the prices of our products must have been somewhat unfavorably affected by these causes, we have escaped a revulsion, our money market is comparatively easy, and public and private credit have advanced and improved.

It is confidently believed that we have been saved from their effect by the salutary operation of the constitutional treasury. It is certain that if the twenty-four millions of specie imported into the country during the fiscal year ending on the 30th of June, 1847, had gone into the banks, as to a great extent it must have done, it would in the absence of this system have been made the basis of augmented bank paper issues, probably to an amount not less than $60,000,000 or $70,000,000, producing, as an inevitable consequence of an inflated currency, extravagant prices for a time and wild speculation, which must have been followed, on the reflux to Europe the succeeding year of so much of that specie, by the prostration of the business of the country, the suspension of the banks, and most extensive bankruptcies. Occurring, as this would have done, at a period when the country was engaged in a foreign war, when considerable loans of specie were required for distant disbursements, and when the banks, the fiscal agents of the Government and the depositories of its money, were suspended, the public credit must have sunk, and many millions of dollars, as was the case during the War of 1812, must have been sacrificed in discounts upon loans and upon the depreciated paper currency which the Government would have been compelled to use.

Under the operations of the constitutional treasury not a dollar has been lost by the depreciation of the currency. The loans required to prosecute the war with Mexico were negotiated by the Secretary of the Treasury above par, realizing a large premium to the Government. The restraining effect of the system upon the tendencies to excessive paper issues by banks has saved the Government from heavy losses and thousands of our business men from bankruptcy and ruin. The wisdom of the system has been tested by the experience of the last two years, and it is the dictate of sound policy that it should remain undisturbed. The modifications in some of the details of this measure, involving none of its essential principles, heretofore recommended, are again presented for your favorable consideration.

In my message of the 6th of July last, transmitting to Congress the ratified treaty of peace with Mexico, I recommended the adoption of measures for the speedy payment of the public debt. In reiterating that recommendation I refer you to the considerations presented in that message in its support. The public debt, including that authorized to be negotiated in pursuance of existing laws, and including Treasury notes, amounted at that time to $65,778,450.41.

Funded stock of the United States amounting to about half a million of dollars has been purchased, as authorized by law, since that period, and the public debt has thus been reduced, the details of which will be presented in the annual report of the Secretary of the Treasury.

The estimates of expenditures for the next fiscal year, submitted by the Secretary of the Treasury, it is believed will be ample for all necessary purposes. If the appropriations made by Congress shall not exceed the amount estimated, the means in the Treasury will be sufficient to defray all the expenses of the Government, to pay off the next installment of $3,000,000 to Mexico, which will fall due on the 30th of May next, and still a considerable surplus will remain, which should be applied to the further purchase of the public stock and reduction of the debt. Should enlarged appropriations be made, the necessary consequence will be to postpone the payment of the debt. Though our debt, as compared with that of most other nations, is small, it is our true policy, and in harmony with the genius of our institutions, that we should present to the world the rare spectacle of a great Republic, possessing vast resources and wealth, wholly exempt from public indebtedness. This would add still more to our strength, and give to us a still more commanding position among the nations of the earth.

The public expenditures should be economical, and be confined to such necessary objects as are clearly within the powers of Congress. All such as are not absolutely demanded should be postponed, and the payment of the public debt at the earliest practicable period should be a cardinal principle of our public policy.

For the reason assigned in my last annual message, I repeat the recommendation that a branch of the Mint of the United States be established at the city of New York. The importance of this measure is greatly increased by the acquisition of the rich mines of the precious metals in New Mexico and California, and especially in the latter.

I repeat the recommendation heretofore made in favor of the graduation and reduction of the price of such of the public lands as have been long offered in the market and have remained unsold, and in favor of extending the rights of preemption to actual settlers on the unsurveyed as well as the surveyed lands.

The condition and operations of the Army and the state of other branches of the public service under the supervision of the War Department are satisfactorily presented in the accompanying report of the Secretary of War.

On the return of peace our forces were withdrawn from Mexico, and the volunteers and that portion of the Regular Army engaged for the war were disbanded. Orders have been issued for stationing the forces of our permanent establishment at various positions in our extended country where troops may be required. Owing to the remoteness of some of these positions, the detachments have not yet reached their destination. Notwithstanding the extension of the limits of our country and the forces required in the new territories, it is confidently believed that our present military establishment is sufficient for all exigencies so long as our peaceful relations remain undisturbed.

Of the amount of military contributions collected in Mexico, the sum of $769,650 was applied toward the payment of the first installment due under the treaty with Mexico. The further sum of $346,369.30 has been paid into the Treasury, and unexpended balances still remain in the hands of disbursing officers and those who were engaged in the collection of these moneys. After the proclamation of peace no further disbursements were made of any unexpended moneys arising from this source. The balances on hand were directed to be paid into the Treasury, and individual claims on the fund will remain unadjusted until Congress shall authorize their settlement and payment. These claims are not considerable in number or amount.

I recommend to your favorable consideration the suggestions of the Secretary of War and the Secretary of the Navy in regard to legislation on this subject.

Our Indian relations are presented in a most favorable view in the report from the War Department. The wisdom of our policy in regard to the tribes within our limits is clearly manifested by their improved and rapidly improving condition.

A most important treaty with the Menomonies has been recently negotiated by the Commissioner of Indian Affairs in person, by which all their land in the State of Wisconsin-being about 4,000,000 acres-has been ceded to the United States. This treaty will be submitted to the Senate for ratification at an early period of your present session.

Within the last four years eight important treaties have been negotiated with different Indian tribes, and at a cost of $1,842,000; Indian lands to the amount of more than 18,500,000 acres have been ceded to the United States, and provision has been made for settling in the country west of the Mississippi the tribes which occupied this large extent of the public domain. The title to all the Indian lands within the several States of our Union, with the exception of a few small reservations, is now extinguished, and a vast region opened for settlement and cultivation.

The accompanying report of the Secretary of the Navy gives a satisfactory exhibit of the operations and condition of that branch of the public service.

A number of small vessels, suitable for entering the mouths of rivers, were judiciously purchased during the war, and gave great efficiency to the squadron in the Gulf of Mexico. On the return of peace, when no longer valuable for naval purposes, and liable to constant deterioration, they were sold and the money placed in the Treasury.

The number of men in the naval service authorized by law during the war has been reduced by discharges below the maximum fixed for the peace establishment. Adequate squadrons are maintained in the several quarters of the globe where experience has shown their services may be most usefully employed, and the naval service was never in a condition of higher discipline or greater efficiency.

I invite attention to the recommendation of the Secretary of the Navy on the subject of the Marine Corps. The reduction of the Corps at the end of the war required that four officers of each of the three lower grades should be dropped from the rolls. A board of officers made the selection, and those designated were necessarily dismissed, but without any alleged fault. I concur in opinion with the Secretary that the service would be improved by reducing the number of landsmen and increasing the marines. Such a measure would justify an increase of the number of officers to the extent of the reduction by dismissal, and still the Corps would have fewer officers than a corresponding number of men in the Army.

The contracts for the transportation of the mail in steamships, convertible into war steamers, promise to realize all the benefits to our commerce and to the Navy which were anticipated. The first steamer thus secured to the Government was launched in January, 1847. There are now seven, and in another year there will probably be not less than seventeen afloat. While this great national advantage is secured, our social and commercial intercourse is increased and promoted with Germany, Great Britain, and other parts of Europe, with all the countries on the west coast of our continent, especially with Oregon and California, and between the northern and southern sections of the United States. Considerable revenue may be expected from postages, but the connected line from New York to Chagres, and thence across the Isthmus to Oregon, can not fail to exert a beneficial influence, not now to be estimated, on the interests of the manufactures, commerce, navigation, and currency of the United States. As an important part of the system, I recommend to your favorable consideration the establishment of the proposed line of steamers between New Orleans and Vera Cruz. It promises the most happy results in cementing friendship between the two Republics and extending reciprocal benefits to the trade and manufactures of both.

The report of the Postmaster-General will make known to you the operations of that Department for the past year.

It is gratifying to find the revenues of the Department, under the rates of postage now established by law, so rapidly increasing. The gross amount of postages during the last fiscal year amounted to $4,371,077, exceeding the annual average received for the nine years immediately preceding the passage of the act of the 3d of March, 1845, by the sum of $6,453, and exceeding the amount received for the year ending the 30th of June, 1847, by the sum of $425,184.

The expenditures for the year, excluding the sum of $94,672, allowed by Congress at its last session to individual claimants, and including the sum of $100,500, paid for the services of the line of steamers between Bremen and New York, amounted to $4,198,845, which is less than the annual average for the nine years previous to the act of 1845 by $300,748.

The mail routes on the 30th day of June last were 163,208 miles in extent, being an increase during the last year of 9,390 miles. The mails were transported over them during the same time 41,012,579 miles, making an increase of transportation for the year of 2,124,680 miles, whilst the expense was less than that of the previous year by $4,235.

The increase in the mail transportation within the last three years has been 5,378,310 miles, whilst the expenses were reduced $456,738, making an increase of service at the rate of 15 per cent and a reduction in the expenses of more than 15 per cent.

During the past year there have been employed, under contracts with the Post-Office Department, two ocean steamers in conveying the mails monthly between New York and Bremen, and one, since October last, performing semimonthly service between Charleston and Havana; and a contract has been made for the transportation of the Pacific mails across the Isthmus from Chagres to Panama.

Under the authority given to the Secretary of the Navy, three ocean steamers have been constructed and sent to the Pacific, and are expected to enter upon the mail service between Panama and Oregon and the intermediate ports on the 1st of January next; and a fourth has been engaged by him for the service between Havana and Chagres, so that a regular monthly mail line will be kept up after that time between the United States and our territories on the Pacific.

Notwithstanding this great increase in the mail service, should the revenue continue to increase the present year as it did in the last, there will be received near $450,000 more than the expenditures.

These considerations have satisfied the Postmaster-General that, with certain modifications of the act of 1845, the revenue may be still further increased and a reduction of postages made to a uniform rate of 5 cents, without an interference with the principle, which has been constantly and properly enforced, of making that Department sustain itself.

A well-digested cheap-postage system is the best means of diffusing intelligence among the people, and is of so much importance in a country so extensive as that of the United States that I recommend to your favorable consideration the suggestions of the Postmaster-General for its improvement.

Nothing can retard the onward progress of our country and prevent us from assuming and maintaining the first rank among nations but a disregard of the experience of the past and a recurrence to an unwise public policy. We have just closed a foreign war by an honorable peace-a war rendered necessary and unavoidable in vindication of the national rights and honor. The present condition of the country is similar in some respects to that which existed immediately after the close of the war with Great Britain in 1815, and the occasion is deemed to be a proper one to take a retrospect of the measures of public policy which followed that war. There was at that period of our history a departure from our earlier policy. The enlargement of the powers of the Federal Government by construction, which obtained, was not warranted by any just interpretation of the Constitution. A few years after the close of that war a series of measures was adopted which, united and combined, constituted what was termed by their authors and advocates the "American system."

The introduction of the new policy was for a time favored by the condition of the country, by the heavy debt which had been contracted during the war, by the depression of the public credit, by the deranged state of the finances and the currency, and by the commercial and pecuniary embarrassment which extensively prevailed. These were not the only causes which led to its establishment. The events of the war with Great Britain and the embarrassments which had attended its prosecution had left on the minds of many of our statesmen the impression that our Government was not strong enough, and that to wield its resources successfully in great emergencies, and especially in war, more power should be concentrated in its hands. This increased power they did not seek to obtain by the legitimate and prescribed mode-an amendment of the Constitution-but by construction. They saw Governments in the Old World based upon different orders of society, and so constituted as to throw the whole power of nations into the hands of a few, who taxed and controlled the many without responsibility or restraint. In that arrangement they conceived the strength of nations in war consisted. There was also something fascinating in the ease, luxury, and display of the higher orders, who drew their wealth from the toil of the laboring millions. The authors of the system drew their ideas of political economy from what they had witnessed in Europe, and particularly in Great Britain. They had viewed the enormous wealth concentrated in few hands and had seen the splendor of the overgrown establishments of an aristocracy which was upheld by the restrictive policy. They forgot to look down upon the poorer classes of the English population, upon whose daily and yearly labor the great establishments they so much admired were sustained and supported. They failed to perceive that the scantily fed and half-clad operatives were not only in abject poverty, but were bound in chains of oppressive servitude for the benefit of favored classes, who were the exclusive objects of the care of the Government.

It was not possible to reconstruct society in the United States upon the European plan. Here there was a written Constitution, by which orders and titles were not recognized or tolerated. A system of measures was therefore devised, calculated, if not intended, to withdraw power gradually and silently from the States and the mass of the people, and by construction to approximate our Government to the European models, substituting an aristocracy of wealth for that of orders and titles.

Without reflecting upon the dissimilarity of our institutions and of the condition of our people and those of Europe, they conceived the vain idea of building up in the United States a system similar to that which they admired abroad. Great Britain had a national bank of large capital, in whose hands was concentrated the controlling monetary and financial power of the nation-an institution wielding almost kingly power, and exerting vast influence upon all the operations of trade and upon the policy of the Government itself. Great Britain had an enormous public debt, and it had become a part of her public policy to regard this as a "public blessing." Great Britain had also a restrictive policy, which placed fetters and burdens on trade and trammeled the productive industry of the mass of the nation. By her combined system of policy the landlords and other property holders were protected and enriched by the enormous taxes which were levied upon the labor of the country for their advantage. Imitating this foreign policy, the first step in establishing the new system in the United States was the creation of a national bank. Not foreseeing the dangerous power and countless evils which such an institution might entail on the country, nor perceiving the connection which it was designed to form between the bank and the other branches of the miscalled "American system," but feeling the embarrassments of the Treasury and of the business of the country consequent upon the war, some of our statesmen who had held different and sounder views were induced to yield their scruples and, indeed, settled convictions of its unconstitutionality, and to give it their sanction as an expedient which they vainly hoped might produce relief. It was a most unfortunate error, as the subsequent history and final catastrophe of that dangerous and corrupt institution have abundantly proved. The bank, with its numerous branches ramified into the States, soon brought many of the active political and commercial men in different sections of the country into the relation of debtors to it and dependents upon it for pecuniary favors, thus diffusing throughout the mass of society a great number of individuals of power and influence to give tone to public opinion and to act in concert in cases of emergency. The corrupt power of such a political engine is no longer a matter of speculation, having been displayed in numerous instances, but most signally in the political struggles of 1832, 1833, and 1834 in opposition to the public will represented by a fearless and patriotic President.

But the bank was but one branch of the new system. A public debt of more than $120,000,000 existed, and it is not to be disguised that many of the authors of the new system did not regard its speedy payment as essential to the public prosperity, but looked upon its continuance as no national evil. Whilst the debt existed it furnished aliment to the national bank and rendered increased taxation necessary to the amount of the interest, exceeding $7,000,000 annually.

This operated in harmony with the next branch of the new system, which was a high protective tariff. This was to afford bounties to favored classes and particular pursuits at the expense of all others. A proposition to tax the whole people for the purpose of enriching a few was too monstrous to be openly made. The scheme was therefore veiled under the plausible but delusive pretext of a measure to protect "home industry," and many of our people were for a time led to believe that a tax which in the main fell upon labor was for the benefit of the laborer who paid it. This branch of the system involved a partnership between the Government and the favored classes, the former receiving the proceeds of the tax imposed on articles imported and the latter the increased price of similar articles produced at home, caused by such tax. It is obvious that the portion to be received by the favored classes would, as a general rule, be increased in proportion to the increase of the rates of tax imposed and diminished as those rates were reduced to the revenue standard required by the wants of the Government. The rates required to produce a sufficient revenue for the ordinary expenditures of Government for necessary purposes were not likely to give to the private partners in this scheme profits sufficient to satisfy their cupidity, and hence a variety of expedients and pretexts were resorted to for the purpose of enlarging the expenditures and thereby creating a necessity for keeping up a high protective tariff. The effect of this policy was to interpose artificial restrictions upon the natural course of the business and trade of the country, and to advance the interests of large capitalists and monopolists at the expense of the great mass of the people, who were taxed to increase their wealth.

Another branch of this system was a comprehensive scheme of internal improvements, capable of indefinite enlargement and sufficient to swallow up as many millions annually as could be exacted from the foreign commerce of the country. This was a convenient and necessary adjunct of the protective tariff. It was to be the great absorbent of any surplus which might at any time accumulate in the Treasury and of the taxes levied on the people, not for necessary revenue purposes, but for the avowed object of affording protection to the favored classes.

Auxiliary to the same end, if it was not an essential part of the system itself, was the scheme, which at a later period obtained, for distributing the proceeds of the sales of the public lands among the States. Other expedients were devised to take money out of the Treasury and prevent its coming in from any other source than the protective tariff. The authors and supporters of the system were the advocates of the largest expenditures, whether for necessary or useful purposes or not, because the larger the expenditures the greater was the pretext for high taxes in the form of protective duties.

These several measures were sustained by popular names and plausible arguments, by which thousands were deluded. The bank was represented to be an indispensable fiscal agent for the Government; was to equalize exchanges and to regulate and furnish a sound currency, always and everywhere of uniform value. The protective tariff was to give employment to "American labor" at advanced prices; was to protect "home industry" and furnish a steady market for the farmer. Internal improvements were to bring trade into every neighborhood and enhance the value of every man's property. The distribution of the land money was to enrich the States, finish their public works, plant schools throughout their borders, and relieve them from taxation. But the fact that for every dollar taken out of the Treasury for these objects a much larger sum was transferred from the pockets of the people to the favored classes was carefully concealed, as was also the tendency, if not the ultimate design, of the system to build up an aristocracy of wealth, to control the masses of society, and monopolize the political power of the country.

The several branches of this system were so intimately blended together that in their operation each sustained and strengthened the others. Their joint operation was to add new burthens of taxation and to encourage a largely increased and wasteful expenditure of public money. It was the interest of the bank that the revenue collected and the disbursements made by the Government should be large, because, being the depository of the public money, the larger the amount the greater would be the bank profits by its use. It was the interest of the favored classes, who were enriched by the protective tariff, to have the rates of that protection as high as possible, for the higher those rates the greater would be their advantage. It was the interest of the people of all those sections and localities who expected to be benefited by expenditures for internal improvements that the amount collected should be as large as possible, to the end that the sum disbursed might also be the larger. The States, being the beneficiaries in the distribution of the land money, had an interest in having the rates of tax imposed by the protective tariff large enough to yield a sufficient revenue from that source to meet the wants of the Government without disturbing or taking from them the land fund; so that each of the branches constituting the system had a common interest in swelling the public expenditures. They had a direct interest in maintaining the public debt unpaid and increasing its amount, because this would produce an annual increased drain upon the Treasury to the amount of the interest and render augmented taxes necessary. The operation and necessary effect of the whole system were to encourage large and extravagant expenditures, and thereby to increase the public patronage, and maintain a rich and splendid government at the expense of a taxed and impoverished people.

It is manifest that this scheme of enlarged taxation and expenditures, had it continued to prevail, must soon have converted the Government of the Union, intended by its framers to be a plain, cheap, and simple confederation of States, united together for common protection and charged with a few specific duties, relating chiefly to our foreign affairs, into a consolidated empire, depriving the States of their reserved rights and the people of their just power and control in the administration of their Government. In this manner the whole form and character of the Government would be changed, not by an amendment of the Constitution, but by resorting to an unwarrantable and unauthorized construction of that instrument.

The indirect mode of levying the taxes by a duty on imports prevents the mass of the people from readily perceiving the amount they pay, and has enabled the few who are thus enriched, and who seek to wield the political power of the country, to deceive and delude them. Were the taxes collected by a direct levy upon the people, as is the ease in the States, this could not occur.

The whole system was resisted from its inception by many of our ablest statesmen, some of whom doubted its constitutionality and its expediency, while others believed it was in all its branches a flagrant and dangerous infraction of the Constitution.

That a national bank, a protective tariff-levied not to raise the revenue needed, but for protection merely-internal improvements, and the distribution of the proceeds of the sale of the public lands are measures without the warrant of the Constitution would, upon the maturest consideration, seem to be clear. It is remarkable that no one of these measures, involving such momentous consequences, is authorized by any express grant of power in the Constitution. No one of them is "incident to, as being necessary and proper for the execution of, the specific powers" granted by the Constitution. The authority under which it has been attempted to justify each of them is derived from inferences and constructions of the Constitution which its letter and its whole object and design do not warrant. Is it to be conceived that such immense powers would have been left by the framers of the Constitution to mere inferences and doubtful constructions? Had it been intended to confer them on the Federal Government, it is but reasonable to conclude that it would have been done by plain and unequivocal grants. This was not done; but the whole structure of which the "American system" consisted was reared on no other or better foundation than forced implications and inferences of power, which its authors assumed might be deduced by construction from the Constitution.

But it has been urged that the national bank, which constituted so essential a branch of this combined system of measures, was not a new measure, and that its constitutionality had been previously sanctioned, because a bank had been chartered in 1791 and had received the official signature of President Washington. A few facts will show the just weight to which this precedent should be entitled as bearing upon the question of constitutionality.

Great division of opinion upon the subject existed in Congress. It is well known that President Washington entertained serious doubts both as to the constitutionality and expediency of the measure, and while the bill was before him for his official approval or disapproval so great were these doubts that he required "the opinion in writing" of the members of his Cabinet to aid him in arriving at a decision. His Cabinet gave their opinions and were divided upon the subject, General Hamilton being in favor of and Mr. Jefferson and Mr. Randolph being opposed to the constitutionality and expediency of the bank. It is well known also that President Washington retained the bill from Monday, the 14th, when it was presented to him, until Friday, the 25th of February, being the last moment permitted him by the

Constitution to deliberate, when he finally yielded to it his reluctant assent and gave it his signature. It is certain that as late as the 23d of February, being the ninth day after the bill was presented to him, he had arrived at no satisfactory conclusion, for on that day he addressed a note to General Hamilton in which he informs him that "this bill was presented to me by the joint committee of Congress at 12 o'clock on Monday, the 14th instant," and he requested his opinion "to what precise period, by legal interpretation of the Constitution, can the President retain it in his possession before it becomes a law by the lapse of ten days." If the proper construction was that the day on which the bill was presented to the President and the day on which his action was had upon it were both to be counted inclusive, then the time allowed him within which it would be competent for him to return it to the House in which it originated with his objections would expire on Thursday, the 24th of February. General Hamilton on the same day returned an answer, in which he states:

I give it as my opinion that you have ten days exclusive of that on which the bill was delivered to you and Sundays; hence, in the present case if it is returned on Friday it will be in time.

By this construction, which the President adopted, he gained another day for deliberation, and it was not until the 25th of February that he signed the bill, thus affording conclusive proof that he had at last obtained his own consent to sign it not without great and almost insuperable difficulty. Additional light has been recently shed upon the serious doubts which he had on the subject, amounting at one time to a conviction that it was his duty to withhold his approval from the bill. This is found among the manuscript papers of Mr. Madison, authorized to be purchased for the use of the Government by an act of the last session of Congress, and now for the first time accessible to the public. From these papers it appears that President Washington, while he yet held the bank bill in his hands, actually requested Mr. Madison, at that time a member of the House of Representatives, to prepare the draft of a veto message for him. Mr. Madison, at his request, did prepare the draft of such a message, and sent it to him on the 21st of February, 1791. A copy of this original draft, in Mr. Madison's own handwriting, was carefully preserved by him, and is among the papers lately purchased by Congress. It is preceded by a note, written on the same sheet, which is also in Mr. Madison's handwriting, and is as follows:

February 21, 1791.Copy of a paper made out and sent to the President, at his request, to be ready in case his judgment should finally decide against the bill for incorporating a national bank, the bill being then before him.

Among the objections assigned in this paper to the bill, and which were submitted for the consideration of the President, are the following:

I object to the bill, because it is an essential principle of the Government that powers not delegated by the Constitution can not be rightfully exercised; because the power proposed by the bill to be exercised is not expressly delegated, and because I can not satisfy myself that it results from any express power by fair and safe rules of interpretation.

The weight of the precedent of the bank of 1791 and the sanction of the great name of Washington, which has been so often invoked in its support, are greatly weakened by the development of these facts.

The experiment of that bank satisfied the country that it ought not to be continued, and at the end of twenty years Congress refused to recharter it. It would have been fortunate for the country, and saved thousands from bankruptcy and ruin, had our public men of 1816 resisted the temporary pressure of the times upon our financial and pecuniary interests and refused to charter the second bank. Of this the country became abundantly satisfied, and at the close of its twenty years' duration, as in the case of the first bank, it also ceased to exist. Under the repeated blows of President Jackson it reeled and fell, and a subsequent attempt to charter a similar institution was arrested by the veto of President Tyler.

Mr. Madison, in yielding his signature to the charter of 1816, did so upon the ground of the respect due to precedents; and, as he subsequently declared-

The Bank of the United States, though on the original question held to be unconstitutional, received the Executive signature.

It is probable that neither the bank of 1791 nor that of 1816 would have been chartered but for the embarrassments of the Government in its finances, the derangement of the currency, and the pecuniary pressure which existed, the first the consequence of the War of the Revolution and the second the consequence of the War of 1812. Both were resorted to in the delusive hope that they would restore public credit and afford relief to the Government and to the business of the country.

Those of our public men who opposed the whole "American system" at its commencement and throughout its progress foresaw and predicted that it was fraught with incalculable mischiefs and must result in serious injury to the best interests of the country. For a series of years their wise counsels were unheeded, and the system was established. It was soon apparent that its practical operation was unequal and unjust upon different portions of the country and upon the people engaged in different pursuits. All were equally entitled to the favor and protection of the Government. It fostered and elevated the money power and enriched the favored few by taxing labor, and at the expense of the many. Its effect was to "make the rich richer and the poor poorer." Its tendency was to create distinctions in society based on wealth and to give to the favored classes undue control and sway in our Government. It was an organized money power, which resisted the popular will and sought to shape and control the public policy.

Under the pernicious workings of this combined system of measures the country witnessed alternate seasons of temporary apparent prosperity, of sudden and disastrous commercial revulsions, of unprecedented fluctuation of prices and depression of the great interests of agriculture, navigation, and commerce, of general pecuniary suffering, and of final bankruptcy of thousands. After a severe struggle of more than a quarter of a century, the system was overthrown.

The bank has been succeeded by a practical system of finance, conducted and controlled solely by the Government. The constitutional currency has been restored, the public credit maintained unimpaired even in a period of a foreign war, and the whole country has become satisfied that banks, national or State, are not necessary as fiscal agents of the Government. Revenue duties have taken the place of the protective tariff. The distribution of the money derived from the sale of the public lands has been abandoned and the corrupting system of internal improvements, it is hoped, has been effectually checked.

It is not doubted that if this whole train of measures, designed to take wealth from the many and bestow it upon the few, were to prevail the effect would be to change the entire character of the Government. One only danger remains. It is the seductions of that branch of the system which consists in internal improvements, holding out, as it does, inducements to the people of particular sections and localities to embark the Government in them without stopping to calculate the inevitable consequences. This branch of the system is so intimately combined and linked with the others that as surely as an effect is produced by an adequate cause, if it be resuscitated and revived and firmly established it requires no sagacity to foresee that it will necessarily and speedily draw after it the reestablishment of a national bank, the revival of a protective tariff, the distribution of the land money, and not only the postponement to the distant future of the payment of the present national debt, but its annual increase.

I entertain the solemn conviction that if the internal-improvement branch of the "American system" be not firmly resisted at this time the whole series of measures composing it will be speedily reestablished and the country be thrown back from its present high state of prosperity, which the existing policy has produced, and be destined again to witness all the evils, commercial revulsions, depression of prices, and pecuniary embarrassments through which we have passed during the last twenty-five years.

To guard against consequences so ruinous is an object of high national importance, involving, in my judgment, the continued prosperity of the country.

I have felt it to be an imperative obligation to withhold my constitutional sanction from two bills which had passed the two Houses of Congress, involving the principle of the internal improvement branch of the "American system" and conflicting in their provisions with the views here expressed.

This power, conferred upon the President by the Constitution, I have on three occasions during my administration of the executive department of the Government deemed it my duty to exercise, and on this last occasion of making to Congress an annual communication "of the state of the Union" it is not deemed inappropriate to review the principles and considerations which have governed my action. I deem this the more necessary because, after the lapse of nearly sixty years since the adoption of the Constitution, the propriety of the exercise of this undoubted constitutional power by the President has for the first time been drawn seriously in question by a portion of my fellow-citizens.

The Constitution provides that- Every bill which shall have passed the House of Representatives and the Senate shall, before it become a law, be presented to the President of the United States. If he approve he shall sign it, but if not he shall return it with his objections to that House in which it shall have originated, who shall enter the objections at large on their Journal and proceed to reconsider it.

The preservation of the Constitution from infraction is the President's highest duty. He is bound to discharge that duty at whatever hazard of incurring the displeasure of those who may differ with him in opinion. He is bound to discharge it as well by his obligations to the people who have clothed him with his exalted trust as by his oath of office, which he may not disregard. Nor are the obligations of the President in any degree lessened by the prevalence of views different from his own in one or both Houses of Congress. It is not alone hasty and inconsiderate legislation that he is required to check; but if at any time Congress shall, after apparently full deliberation, resolve on measures which he deems subversive of the Constitution or of the vital interests of the country, it is his solemn duty to stand in the breach and resist them. The President is bound to approve or disapprove every bill which passes Congress and is presented to him for his signature. The Constitution makes this his duty, and he can not escape it if he would. He has no election. In deciding upon any bill presented to him he must exercise his own best judgment. If he can not approve, the Constitution commands him to return the bill to the House in which it originated with his objections, and if he fail to do this within ten days (Sundays excepted) it shall become a law without his signature. Right or wrong, he may be overruled by a vote of two-thirds of each House, and in that event the bill becomes a law without his sanction. If his objections be not thus overruled, the subject is only postponed, and is referred to the States and the people for their consideration and decision. The President's power is negative merely, and not affirmative. He can enact no law. The only effect, therefore, of his withholding his approval of a bill passed by Congress is to suffer the existing laws to remain unchanged, and the delay occasioned is only that required to enable the States and the people to consider and act upon the subject in the election of public agents who will carry out their wishes and instructions. Any attempt to coerce the President to yield his sanction to measures which he can not approve would be a violation of the spirit of the Constitution, palpable and flagrant, and if successful would break down the independence of the executive department and make the President, elected by the people and clothed by the Constitution with power to defend their rights, the mere instrument of a majority of Congress. A surrender on his part of the powers with which the Constitution has invested his office would effect a practical alteration of that instrument without resorting to the prescribed process of amendment.

With the motives or considerations which may induce Congress to pass any bill the President can have nothing to do. He must presume them to be as pure as his own, and look only to the practical effect of their measures when compared with the Constitution or the public good.

But it has been urged by those who object to the exercise of this undoubted constitutional power that it assails the representative principle and the capacity of the people to govern themselves; that there is greater safety in a numerous representative body than in the single Executive created by the Constitution, and that the Executive veto is a "one-man power," despotic in its character. To expose the fallacy of this objection it is only necessary to consider the frame and true character of our system. Ours is not a consolidated empire, but a confederated union. The States before the adoption of the Constitution were coordinate, co-equal, and separate independent sovereignties, and by its adoption they did not lose that character. They clothed the Federal Government with certain powers and reserved all others, including their own sovereignty, to themselves. They guarded their own rights as States and the rights of the people by the very limitations which they incorporated into the Federal Constitution, whereby the different departments of the General Government were checks upon each other. That the majority should govern is a general principle controverted by none, but they must govern according to the Constitution, and not according to an undefined and unrestrained discretion, whereby they may oppress the minority.

The people of the United States are not blind to the fact that they may be temporarily misled, and that their representatives, legislative and executive, may be mistaken or influenced in their action by improper motives. They have therefore interposed between themselves and the laws which may be passed by their public agents various representations, such as assemblies, senates, and governors in their several States, a House of Representatives, a Senate, and a President of the United States. The people can by their own direct agency make no law, nor can the House of Representatives, immediately elected by them, nor can the Senate, nor can both together without the concurrence of the President or a vote of two-thirds of both Houses.

Happily for themselves, the people in framing our admirable system of government were conscious of the infirmities of their representatives, and in delegating to them the power of legislation they have fenced them around with checks to guard against the effects of hasty action, of error, of combination, and of possible corruption. Error, selfishness, and faction have often sought to rend asunder this web of checks and subject the Government to the control of fanatic and sinister influences, but these efforts have only satisfied the people of the wisdom of the checks which they have imposed and of the necessity of preserving them unimpaired.

The true theory of our system is not to govern by the acts or decrees of any one set of representatives. The Constitution interposes checks upon all branches of the Government, in order to give time for error to be corrected and delusion to pass away; but if the people settle down into a firm conviction different from that of their representatives they give effect to their opinions by changing their public servants. The checks which the people imposed on their public servants in the adoption of the Constitution are the best evidence of their capacity for self-government. They know that the men whom they elect to public stations are of like infirmities and passions with themselves, and not to be trusted without being restricted by coordinate authorities and constitutional limitations. Who that has witnessed the legislation of Congress for the last thirty years will say that he knows of no instance in which measures not demanded by the public good have been carried ? Who will deny that in the State governments, by combinations of individuals and sections, in derogation of the general interest, banks have been chartered, systems of internal improvements adopted, and debts entailed upon the people repressing their growth and impairing their energies for years to come?

After so much experience it can not be said that absolute unchecked power is safe in the hands of any one set of representatives, or that the capacity of the people for self-government, which is admitted in its broadest extent, is a conclusive argument to prove the prudence, wisdom, and integrity of their representatives.

The people, by the Constitution, have commanded the President, as much as they have commanded the legislative branch of the Government, to execute their will. They have said to him in the Constitution, which they require he shall take a solemn oath to support, that if Congress pass any bill which he can not approve "he shall return it to the House in which it originated with his objections." In withholding from it his approval and signature he is executing the will of the people, constitutionally expressed, as much as the Congress that passed it. No bill is presumed to be in accordance with the popular will until it shall have passed through all the branches of the Government required by the Constitution to make it a law. A bill which passes the House of Representatives may be rejected by the Senate, and so a bill passed by the Senate may be rejected by the House. In each case the respective Houses exercise the veto power on the other.

Congress, and each House of Congress, hold under the Constitution a check upon the President, and he, by the power of the qualified veto, a check upon Congress. When the President recommends measures to Congress, he avows in the most solemn form his opinions, gives his voice in their favor, and pledges himself in advance to approve them if passed by Congress. If he acts without due consideration, or has been influenced by improper or corrupt motives, or if from any other cause Congress, or either House of Congress, shall differ with him in opinion, they exercise their veto upon his recommendations and reject them; and there is no appeal from their decision but to the people at the ballot box. These are proper checks upon the Executive, wisely interposed by the Constitution. None will be found to object to them or to wish them removed. It is equally important that the constitutional checks of the Executive upon the legislative branch should be preserved.

If it be said that the Representatives in the popular branch of Congress are chosen directly by the people, it is answered, the people elect the President. If both Houses represent the States and the people, so does the President. The President represents in the executive department the whole people of the United States, as each member of the legislative department represents portions of them.

The doctrine of restriction upon legislative and executive power, while a well-settled public opinion is enabled within a reasonable time to accomplish its ends, has made our country what it is, and has opened to us a career of glory and happiness to which all other nations have been strangers.

In the exercise of the power of the veto the President is responsible not only to an enlightened public opinion, but to the people of the whole Union, who elected him, as the representatives in the legislative branches who differ with him in opinion are responsible to the people of particular States or districts, who compose their respective constituencies. To deny to the President the exercise of this power would be to repeal that provision of the Constitution which confers it upon him. To charge that its exercise unduly controls the legislative will is to complain of the Constitution itself.

If the Presidential veto be objected to upon the ground that it checks and thwarts the popular will, upon the same principle the equality of representation of the States in the Senate should be stricken out of the Constitution. The vote of a Senator from Delaware has equal weight in deciding upon the most important measures with the vote of a Senator from New York, and yet the one represents a State containing, according to the existing apportionment of Representatives in the House of Representatives, but one thirty-fourth part of the population of the other. By the constitutional composition of the Senate a majority of that body from the smaller States represent less than one-fourth of the people of the Union. There are thirty States, and under the existing apportionment of Representatives there are 230 Members in the House of Representatives. Sixteen of the smaller States are represented in that House by but 50 Members, and yet the Senators from these States constitute a majority of the Senate. So that the President may recommend a measure to Congress, and it may receive the sanction and approval of more than three-fourths of the House of Representatives and of all the Senators from the large States, containing more than three-fourths of the whole population of the United States, and yet the measure may be defeated by the votes of the Senators from the smaller States. None, it is presumed, can be found ready to change the organization of the Senate on this account, or to strike that body practically out of existence by requiring that its action shall be conformed to the will of the more numerous branch.

Upon the same principle that the veto of the President should be practically abolished the power of the Vice-President to give the casting vote upon an equal division of the Senate should be abolished also. The Vice-President exercises the veto power as effectually by rejecting a bill by his casting vote as the President does by refusing to approve and sign it. This power has been exercised by the Vice-President in a few instances, the most important of which was the rejection of the bill to recharter the Bank of the United States in 1811. It may happen that a bill may be passed by a large majority of the House of Representatives, and may be supported by the Senators from the larger States, and the Vice-President may reject it by giving his vote with the Senators from the smaller States; and yet none, it is presumed, are prepared to deny to him the exercise of this power under the Constitution.

But it is, in point of fact, untrue that an act passed by Congress is conclusive evidence that it is an emanation of the popular will. A majority of the whole number elected to each House of Congress constitutes a quorum, and a majority of that quorum is competent to pass laws. It might happen that a quorum of the House of Representatives, consisting of a single member more than half of the whole number elected to that House, might pass a bill by a majority of a single vote, and in that case a fraction more than one-fourth of the people of the United States would be represented by those who voted for it. It might happen that the same bill might be passed by a majority of one of a quorum of the Senate, composed of Senators from the fifteen smaller States and a single Senator from a sixteenth State; and if the Senators voting for it happened to be from the eight of the smallest of these States, it would be passed by the votes of Senators from States having but fourteen Representatives in the House of Representatives, and containing less than one-sixteenth of the whole population of the United States. This extreme case is stated to illustrate the fact that the mere passage of a bill by Congress is no conclusive evidence that those who passed it represent the majority of the people of the United States or truly reflect their will. If such an extreme case is not likely to happen, cases that approximate it are of constant occurrence. It is believed that not a single law has been passed since the adoption of the Constitution upon which all the members elected to both Houses have been present and voted. Many of the most important acts which have passed Congress have been carried by a close vote in thin Houses. Many instances of this might be given. Indeed, our experience proves that many of the most important acts of Congress are postponed to the last days, and often the last hours, of a session, when they are disposed of in haste, and by Houses but little exceeding the number necessary to form a quorum.

Besides, in most of the States the members of the House of Representatives are chosen by pluralities, and not by majorities of all the voters in their respective districts, and it may happen that a majority of that House may be returned by a less aggregate vote of the people than that received by the minority.

If the principle insisted on be sound, then the Constitution should be so changed that no bill shall become a law unless it is voted for by members representing in each House a majority of the whole people of the United States. We must remodel our whole system, strike down and abolish not only the salutary checks lodged in the executive branch, but must strike out and abolish those lodged in the Senate also, and thus practically invest the whole power of the Government in a majority of a single assembly-a majority uncontrolled and absolute, and which may become despotic. To conform to this doctrine of the right of majorities to rule, independent of the checks and limitations of the Constitution, we must revolutionize our whole system; we must destroy the constitutional compact by which the several States agreed to form a Federal Union and rush into consolidation, which must end in monarchy or despotism. No one advocates such a proposition, and yet the doctrine maintained, if carried out, must lead to this result.

One great object of the Constitution in conferring upon the President a qualified negative upon the legislation of Congress was to protect minorities from injustice and oppression by majorities. The equality of their representation in the Senate and the veto power of the President are the constitutional guaranties which the smaller States have that their rights will be respected. Without these guaranties all their interests would be at the mercy of majorities in Congress representing the larger States. To the smaller and weaker States, therefore, the preservation of this power and its exercise upon proper occasions demanding it is of vital importance. They ratified the Constitution and entered into the Union, securing to themselves an equal representation with the larger States in the Senate; and they agreed to be bound by all laws passed by Congress upon the express condition, and none other, that they should be approved by the President or passed, his objections to the contrary notwithstanding, by a vote of two-thirds of both Houses. Upon this condition they have a right to insist as a part of the compact to which they gave their assent.

A bill might be passed by Congress against the will of the whole people of a particular State and against the votes of its Senators and all its Representatives. However prejudicial it might be to the interests of such State, it would be bound by it if the President shall approve it or it shall be passed by a vote of two-thirds of both Houses; but it has a right to demand that the President shall exercise his constitutional power and arrest it if his judgment is against it. If he surrender this power, or fail to exercise it in a case where he can not approve, it would make his formal approval a mere mockery, and would be itself a violation of the Constitution, and the dissenting State would become bound by a law which had not been passed according to the sanctions of the Constitution.

The objection to the exercise of the veto power is founded upon an idea respecting the popular will, which, if carried out, would annihilate State sovereignty and substitute for the present Federal Government a consolidation directed by a supposed numerical majority. A revolution of the Government would be silently effected and the States would be subjected to laws to which they had never given their constitutional consent.

The Supreme Court of the United States is invested with the power to declare, and has declared, acts of Congress passed with the concurrence of the Senate, the House of Representatives, and the approval of the President to be unconstitutional and void, and yet none, it is presumed, can be found who will be disposed to strip this highest judicial tribunal under the Constitution of this acknowledged power-a power necessary alike to its independence and the rights of individuals.

For the same reason that the Executive veto should, according to the doctrine maintained, be rendered nugatory, and be practically expunged from the Constitution, this power of the court should also be rendered nugatory and be expunged, because it restrains the legislative and Executive will, and because the exercise of such a power by the court may be regarded as being in conflict with the capacity of the people to govern themselves. Indeed, there is more reason for striking this power of the court from the Constitution than there is that of the qualified veto of the president, because the decision of the court is final, and can never be reversed even though both Houses of Congress and the President should be unanimous in opposition to it, whereas the veto of the President may be overruled by a vote of two-thirds of both Houses of Congress or by the people at the polls.

It is obvious that to preserve the system established by the Constitution each of the coordinate branches of the Government-the executive, legislative, and judicial-must be left in the exercise of its appropriate powers. If the executive or the judicial branch be deprived of powers conferred upon either as checks on the legislative, the preponderance of the latter will become disproportionate and absorbing and the others impotent for the accomplishment of the great objects for which they were established. Organized, as they are, by the Constitution, they work together harmoniously for the public good. If the Executive and the judiciary shall be deprived of the constitutional powers invested in them, and of their due proportions, the equilibrium of the system must be destroyed, and consolidation, with the most pernicious results, must ensue-a consolidation of unchecked, despotic power, exercised by majorities of the legislative branch.

The executive, legislative, and judicial each constitutes a separate coordinate department of the Government, and each is independent of the others. In the performance of their respective duties under the Constitution neither can in its legitimate action control the others. They each act upon their several responsibilities in their respective spheres. But if the doctrines now maintained be correct, the executive must become practically subordinate to the legislative, and the judiciary must become subordinate to both the legislative and the executive; and thus the whole power of the Government would be merged in a single department. Whenever, if ever, this shall occur, our glorious system of well-regulated self-government will crumble into ruins, to be succeeded, first by anarchy, and finally by monarchy or despotism. I am far from believing that this doctrine is the sentiment of the American people; and during the short period which remains in which it will be my duty to administer the executive department it will be my aim to maintain its independence and discharge its duties without infringing upon the powers or duties of either of the other departments of the Government.

The power of the Executive veto was exercised by the first and most illustrious of my predecessors and by four of his successors who preceded me in the administration of the Government, and it is believed in no instance prejudicially to the public interests. It has never been and there is but little danger that it ever can be abused. No President will ever desire unnecessarily to place his opinion in opposition to that of Congress. He must always exercise the power reluctantly, and only in cases where his convictions make it a matter of stern duty, which he can not escape. Indeed, there is more danger that the President, from the repugnance he must always feel to come in collision with Congress, may fail to exercise it in cases where the preservation of the Constitution from infraction, or the public good, may demand it than that he will ever exercise it unnecessarily or wantonly.

During the period I have administered the executive department of the Government great and important questions of public policy, foreign and domestic, have arisen, upon which it was my duty to act. It may, indeed, be truly said that my Administration has fallen upon eventful times. I have felt most sensibly the weight of the high responsibilities devolved upon me. With no other object than the public good, the enduring fame, and permanent prosperity of my country, I have pursued the convictions of my own best judgment. The impartial arbitrament of enlightened public opinion, present and future, will determine how far the public policy I have maintained and the measures I have from time to time recommended may have tended to advance or retard the public prosperity at home and to elevate or depress the estimate of our national character abroad.

Invoking the blessings of the Almighty upon your deliberations at your present important session, my ardent hope is that in a spirit of harmony and concord you may be guided to wise results, and such as may redound to the happiness, the honor, and the glory of our beloved country.

www.ingramcontent.com/pod-product-compliance
Lightning Source LLC
Chambersburg PA
CBHW070827290526
45795CB00002B/864